LITVOICE 0

A LITERARY MONTHLY MAGAZINE

LITVOICE

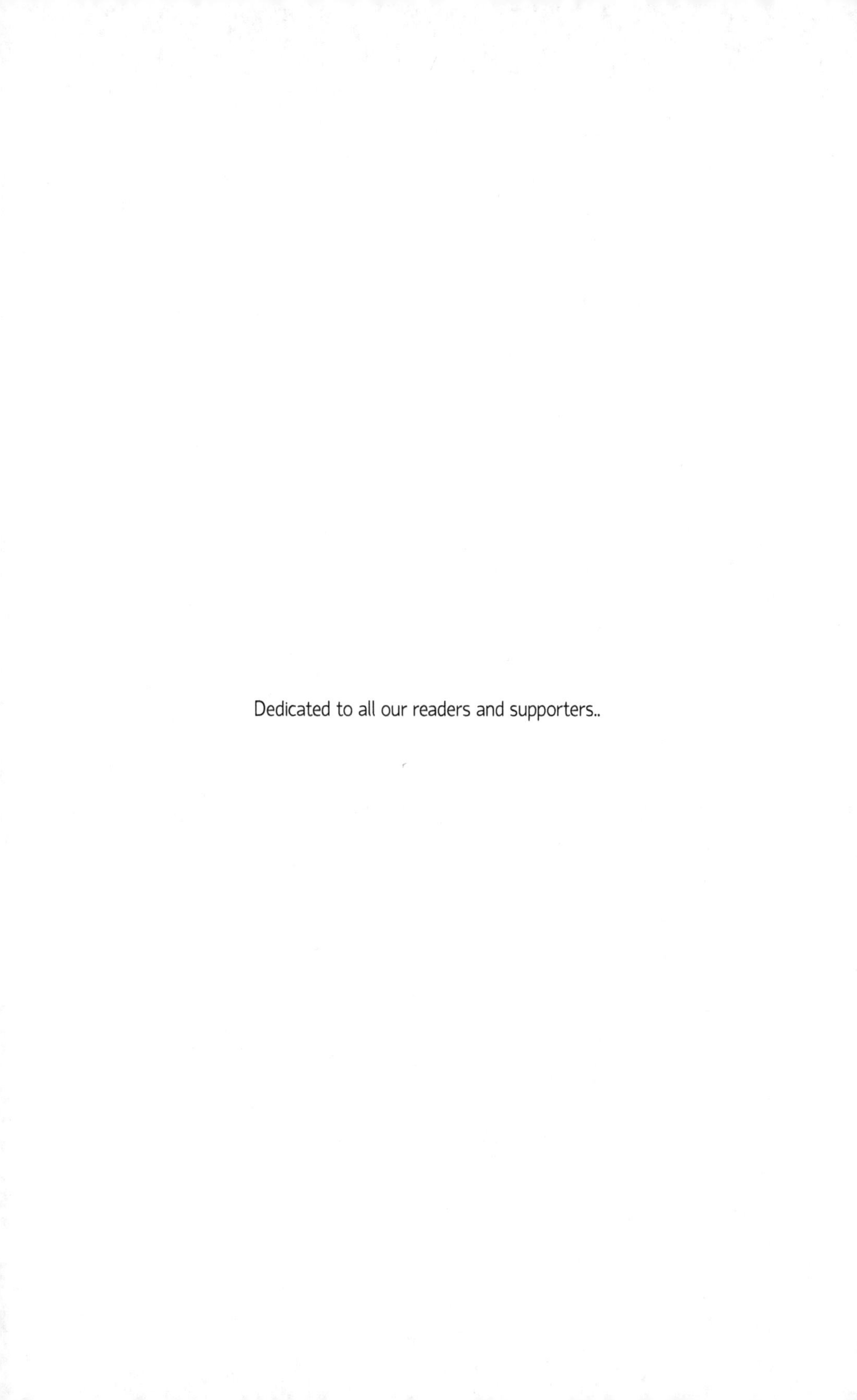

Dedicated to all our readers and supporters..

Contents

Foreword

" Literary voice " is a magazine of young writers. To express and to showcase their talent across the world.

Our own personal grouse with linguistic writing is that a great deal of it is far too technical for

(1) A general reader and

(2) A reader who doesn't want to fall asleep.

This is symptomatic of academic writing as a whole, of course; but that implies just how much of linguistics remains difficult to access if you don't have the requisite training and vocabulary (whose required level of familiarity sometimes boggles the mind).

I think a lot of what happens in linguistics is really, really good work that deserves to be recognized and championed for its worth and value to society, and used in multidisciplinary attempts to make the world a better place. Unfortunately, a lot of it can't reach the non-academically inclined person with big ideas because it's difficult to read and make sense of.

Preface

This is our 28ᵗʰ issue of " LitVoice " to reveal the voice of our unrevealed writers and poets...

Our aim is to showcase their unrevaled talent.... It's a passion. A love of words, and sentences, and subjectivities that make us all very much imperfect, and very much human, as we struggle to find words to express what we think and feel.

It remains only for me to thank you, my dear, cherished, highly sought-after reader. Thank you for reading this and supporting us, and I hope you come to love language as much as we do.

Welcome to "LitVoice". Let's reveal the world together...

Acknowledgements

LitVoice . We are Revealing Magazine for all ..now you all must think why this Name .. but " Literary Voice" was a better fit: it collocates nicely with a strong impact, this magazine is just an idea for giving us English Language majors something to do in our spare time. [There's another, even better reason, but I'll let you, the keen-eyed reader, figure it out].....hurray ..lets begin ...

From The Editor's Desk

Dear Reader:

In year 2018, in India, I started a little magazine devoted to fiction, poetry and literature. Firsty named "Literary Voice" then changed into "LitVoice" (Just a shorter version). LitVoice is India's leading bimonthly literary magazine. Since then we have published some of the best authors in and outside the country. Our generation grew up with the literature as a fact of life. India had many other magazine, but not a proper literature magazine to be called. India's literary magazine. To our minds, it is. It has launched our favorite writers. It has made a special claim for the quarterly as such, being both timely and lasting, free of the news of the day or the pressure to please a crowd. Most of all, the LitVoice has shown, repeatedly, that works of imagination can be as stylish and urgent as the flashiest feature reporting, and can do more to refocus our picture of the literature world.

Dedicated. Smart. Fearless. Strong. Eager to change the world. Willing to stay up late and awake before dawn to pursue their passion. Those are just a few words that describe our work at LitVoice Magazine. As my team and I pulled together the articles and writeups, that we think deserve to be shared.

When I read a literary magazine, I like to skip to the meaty insides. So, when it comes to the editor's note, I've always been a little suspicious of the genre. Editing, after all, is an invisible art. The work in this issue matters to me, and I hope it will matter to you. The package and the publicity matter to me too—those details might be part of what brought you here, to this note. My great hope is that you'll click out of here and go read this Issuewith great delight. It really needs no introduction, but it does need engaged readers through which to come alive. And hopefully when you're reading, you'll forget all about me and this note, which means I've done my job.

I think you'll be impressed.

Agrata Shanaya Shukla

Founder/ Chief Editor

CHAPTER ONE

Cover Story – Dr. Shellie Hipsky

Dr. Shellie Hipsky

Dr. Shellie Hipsky is the CEO of Inspiring Lives International, the Executive Director of the Global Sisterhood (which helps women and children around the world), and the editor-in-chief of Inspiring Lives Magazine. The American Chronicle called her "A top entrepreneur in the U.S.," and the Huffington Post categorized her as a "Fierce Woman." Dr.

Shellie has earned the titles of "The Entrepreneur of the Year" and "Best Woman in Business". The former tenured professor, host of Empowering Women Radio, and Inspiring Lives with Dr. Shellie on NBC has keynoted internationally from Passion to Profits in Hollywood to The University of Oxford in England. She has been featured on over 35 magazine covers and on all the major television networks. She frequently writes for Forbes and serves on their Expert Panel of coaches. An award-winning author, she wrote the Common Threads trilogy on Inspiration, Empowerment, and Balance. Her 13th book Ball Gowns to Yoga Pants: Entrepreneurial Secrets to Create Your Dream Business and Brand is an international bestseller. Currently, Dr. Shellie is booking her EmpowerU Master Class and World Class VIP 1:1 coaching clients to inspire women entrepreneurs. Learn more about Dr. Shellie's mission at www.ShellieHipsky.com.

Her Accolades and Awards:

- 2021 "One of the "Top 20 Business Coaches" worldwide – VIP Global Magazine
- 2021 "Top 10 Inspiring Women to Look out for in 2021" – New York Weekly
- 2021 "Outstanding Professional Character Award" from Media – The Creative Agency
- 2021 "Forbes Contributor and Official Member" from the Forbes Coaching Council
- 2021 "Featured Founding Cover Coach" from Six-Figure Women Coaches Magazine
- 2021 "Official Member & Founder" from the Global Sisterhood
- 2021 "Global Ambassador" from the World Heritage Cultural Center
- 2021 "Featured Selection in the World's Best Business Book Club" from C-Suite Book Club
- 2021 "Executive Leader" from the C-Suite Network
- 2020 "The Author Zone Award in Business" from TAZ
- 2020 "Five Star Author & Official Selection" from Bedside Reading
- 2020 "Impact Maker" from Ruchi Singh Talks
- 2019 "Social Legend" award from Real Beauty Real Women
- 2019 "Business Choice" award for Inspiring Lives Magazine from The Pittsburgh Business Show
- 2017 "Women of Achievement" award from Cribs for Kids

- 2015 "Entrepreneur of the Year in Inspiration and Empowerment" from VIP Events Concierge
- 2015 "VIP Woman of the Year Circle" award from the National Association Professional Women
- 2015 "Tenured Associate Professor" from Robert Morris University
- 2014 "Exceptional Artist Award" Pittsburgh Fashion Week – Fashion Hall of Fame
- 2013 "Super Professor" from the Faculty Row
- 2013 "Best Business Woman in Pittsburgh" from the Women's Small Business Association

CHAPTER TWO

Tejaswini Sundar - A Sensational Youth Author

Author Tejaswini Sundar with her book "Sangam"

It wasn't until the age of six that I realized the power an individual's words had on my tiny mind. A stack of children's books lying untouched on our ordinary wooden bookshelf caught my attention; its hard covers still intact after extensive usage. I silently made my way through the clutter of paper andother household valuables to grab one of Enid Blyton's works, proceeding to plop myself on the floor,immersing myself in her narration.

My world came undone as I, like many others, witnessed every scene and conversation, watching it all unfold before my eyes. Her story-telling sent me spinning,while the illustrations served as fuel to my imagination, which now craved more food. Down cameeach book as I flipped through the pages until I felt my fingers brush against the hardcover as I neatly set them aside until small towers of texts partitioned me from reality. I remember my eyes wideningduring a tense scene, my lips forming an O while I wracked my brain for numerous possibilities to findan alternate, befitting ending. My journey into the world of creative writing began that day: a curious,bubbly six-year-old seated comfortably on a nearby couch, dreaming up of scenarios, characters, plottwists, and gritty scenes to either complement or substitute the existing plotline.It is pretty challenging to escape an Indian society's claws, even if you happen to live away from yourmotherland for eighteen years. My interests always lay in the creative arts; I was able to find myselfand embrace factors and aspects of my childhood, culture, and tradition that defined my character traitsand quirks. I associated myself with fictitious beings and settings and secretly mapped out potentialstories that never saw the light of day. Unlike any other Indian kid, I refused to accept subjects like Math and Science; to me, all those topics ever did was shower down my ideas with terms such as "logic," leaving no room for creativity and originality. Belonging to the Southern regions of the Indian subcontinent and living in the Gulf gave me the added advantage of bonding with several communitiesthat introduced me to the nuances of Indian art using music and dance. At age sixteen, I decided topursue the creative arts when I saw my dreams shot down by familial expectations and unspoken yet rigorously followed laws set by said Indian society. My world spun once again, this time by elements of reality, as I rallied myself back on my feet to prepare for an unexpected voyage down the tracks of logic. I documented each of my days not as diary entries but as traits of a character that I wished to embody. Six years in, graduated from MNNIT Allahabad with an Undergraduate degree in Information Technology, bagging a position in the corporate world's HR-IT sector. Although my courseb entailed substantial technical knowledge and understanding, leaving little to no room for creativity, my growing desire to create anything shifted towards the writing sphere. I gradually taught myself to express my thoughts, emotions, and ideas, recapping examples from many fictional authors I came across. This desire grew into a burning fire when an idea struck me in the form of poetry/song. From that day, 19th January 2019, I refused to look back.

I keep mentioning being inspired by authors and eminent personalities who've motivated me to churn out concepts and schemes for a compelling idea. It started with my dearest paternal grandfather, who urged my brother and me to write him hand-written letters, which later evolved to emails describing a recent event, concert, or just the past week. Reading the works of distinguished authors of fiction, such as JK Rowling, JRR Tolkein, George R. R. Martin, Rick Riordan, Amish Tripathi, and Devi Yesodharan, taught me to create an original story with elements of fiction, fantasy, and history, and mythology. Devi's work on the Chola Empire drove me to pen down my ideas, listing them down chronologically to form a pattern from where my novel would begin. I've got many people to thank throughout the road to self-realization, including my family, who later stood by me and supported my decisions, but I owe my new identity to my 2017 self. She lit the spark and marched forward, to which I will forever be grateful. Sangam: The Awakening is just the beginning of a journey I know I'll be thrilled to take.

CHAPTER THREE

SHE - KEERTHI MOSES
(Poem)

Keerthi Moses

The wind blows heavily,
as fragile arms circle the pillar
fingers entwined shake,
forehead furrowed,
She stands.
Her eyes smoothen the vision--
unfurling, searching for a lost dream.

Futile was her ambition
Battling all the tradition
That had built her.
    What churned inside?
Beads of sweat rolled down,
Riding streams her cheeks unwound.
Her eyes blurred;
lost was the dream, forever.
    What churned inside
eluded her gaze, slipping
through the vaults of her mind.
The weight bends her,
binding her to needless reckoning.
    What churned inside
sleep for days, in the recess
of her mind, easing the weight.
Delicately, she stands,
fearing its awakening.
    What churned inside
awoke in the dark,
baring its teeth, laughing.
Crumbling, she stoops,
whilst it violently reigns.
    What churned inside was blind.
Its enchanting grip
shall never reign her in.
She shudders, yet,
stands tall, waiting
to strike.
    She looked up,
the waves crashing within,
sailing through the--
cotton-candy orbs above.
Her dreams weaved in
through the cotton-candy sea.
    She breathed in.
Felt the peace coursing,
through her veins.

She remembered; stronger--
than the churning sea within,
she cruised through time.

Imperfect love – Book Review

About the Author

Jaishree Laxmikant has been writing for the past five years. What started as blogs of simple expressions, soon turned into a passion and she has been writing ever since about many things apart from fiction. She was a working professional, at a senior level but decided to turn into a homemaker to stay close to her growing kids. She loves to read, travel and spend time with her furry baby. She believes that we are all a means to a purpose and we should always help in uplifting each other without belittling ourselves.

Book "Imperfect Love"

Imperfect Love is a collection of thoughts, about love, separation, heartbreak and soul connections. The thoughts are not about one person or one relationship. They may have been felt by anybody who has/ had been in love and had been or has been away from them. They may have moved on yet not been able to forget them or stop loving them. Love is supposed to be divine then why does it need to be defined?

> *"It is easier to deal with*
> *No promises*
> *Than to deal with*
> *The broken ones."*

The poems will bring that knowing smile on our faces, reminding us of the weakest moments of life. One could relate to the poems well. The feeling of unrequited love, not being on the same page, the courage to move on is beautifully expressed by the author. Not to forget the wonderful illustrations for a few poems that adds beauty to the book. The intriguing writing style with simple and strong words makes the best combination that hits the right chord. What we loved most is the simplicity and depth in the author's words. You will Witness the shades of love along with the plethora of emotions. The poems are strong, powerful, and to the point. Overall, it's a light, breezy read that you can opt for. Recommended for beginners too.

Jaishree's Imperfect love is a collection of 86 poems based on love, joy, loss, heartbreak & hope. It not only revolves around these words which describes the entire journey of a man's life rather, words that would express every emotion that is buried in your heart. There is no fixed pattern or agenda behind this poetry collection as every poem has a different theme and give a different message and some sort of a support to it's readers letting them know that they are not alone. These is a certain calm which bounds you to this book and transforms you to the universe of the poetess where you feel what she is feeling. It's gorgeous. It's peaceful. It's naturally loving. You will not want to keep it down. However, I would advise you to read these poems just like you're drinking a glass of wine... slowly

CHAPTER FIVE

Budding Thoughts - Charu Aganpal

Author Charu Aganpal

Growing up, I was an observant introvert. I could say that this gave me the power to be empathetic and to seek out new perspectives of life. I noticed how often small, light-hearted moments of joy were overlooked in our busy lives. We hustled to meet deadlines and make earnings, forgetting that the time we lost and the moments we missed will never come back. With faith in my heart and in God, I began this journey of writing as a humble expression of my thoughts.

This book is written with the hopes of presenting newer perspectives of love, life, and humanity to the readers. As a psychologist and founder of Hope-The Psychology Clinic, and a published author, I believe that patience, consistency, and optimism are crucial to my professional life; and as a true human being, I believe that cherishing the art of attitude and gratitude are central to leading a wholesome personal life. For me, it was always important that I be a good person inside out, and not merely reflect externally. For this, it was essential to transform my frame of mind, which I successfully did by spending time on myself and introspecting.

From a young age, I was inspired to become a writer by seeing authors like Paulo Coelho, Robin Sharma, Rumi, and James Clear being quoted. I dreamed to one day see my name below a quote from my very own book. Following my heart and never giving up on my zeal to achieve heights, I strove hard to climb every mountain- because like I always say, 'no hill is too tough to climb, so see you at top!'

I enjoy including books in my self-care routine, seated with my dogs and a cup of hot coffee. I have quite a hyperactive mind, and I admit that I am guilty of starting one book before I've finished the other!

A pure and empathetic soul, I was always able to feel compassion for everyone around me. The happiness I gained from helping others translates into the stories in the book. The tales of Usha, Mrs. Reena, and Samir leave the reader in a respectful silence while that of Manu is a heart-warming lesson on aiding humanity in the tiniest steps possible. The stories of Trisha and Zubina emanate human strength even in times of great distress. Chetanya and Shaurya's story leaves the reader in spell-bound awe. This collection of short stories was written with an affirmative, positive approach. With this outlook in mind, always remember to take one step at a time- be it a giant leap or a baby step. Budding Thoughts is bound to encourage you to pursue life's meaning with a transformed outlook.

To all my readers, I want to ask you to be patient and to trust your own blueprint. No matter how you start your story, make sure you make the most of it. Like the tales in this little book of positivity, your path is bound to take an affirmative turn. Enjoy this heartening read in your own way!

Lots of love...keep shining!

CHAPTER SIX

Abhay's Suicide Note – Shagnick Bhattacharya

There was a knock on the door. It was the sweeper, like every morning after breakfast. I was still half-asleep, lying in my bed. Subhash, my roommate, opened the door. While I had missed my breakfast today, he had woken up at the same time he gets up everyday, had his breakfast and was now studying at his table,

before he went up to answer the door. In came the sweeper with his broom and a register, and handed the latter, with a pen in it, to Subhash. It was the room cleaning record register, and my roommate

put his signature against today's date, acknowledging the cleaning of the room. This was a boy's hostel where we stayed, in Kirby Place, near the Base Hospital, in Delhi. It was the temporary residence of about a hundred college students of Delhi University. I and Subhash were living in room number 4 of this hostel

together for about a year. Both of us were in the same college in the University – Delhi College of Arts and Commerce. He is in first year History honours, while I am a fresher student of B.Com program. Both of us are Bengalis - he from Calcutta, and I from Barrackpore. Needless to say, we are quite good friends.

The sweeper was done with our room. I requested him to do the bathroom as well.

Subhash Roy aspires to be an Archaeologist. He is a tall, fair, spectacled guy, not very good-looking I might add, a little overweight too. But such ingenuity as he possesses is rarely found in other people of his age. He does not talk to everyone in the hostel out of a notion of superiority, but is well-respected by everyone here owing to his disciplined life, helpful behaviour towards anyone who needs help, as well as a good sense of humour. Oh yes, and I am Bhaskar Chatterjee, of the same height and complexion as his, just physically much more fit than him. I want to become an author, and that is a major reason why I am now writing about my thrilling experience of that day. If you, as my reader, don't believe this account, then I cannot blame you. That human existence is so very transient and that insignificance can still be so

significant is something that I – and most of the people – wouldn't have understood before.

After the sweeper left the room after cleaning, Subhash sat on his chair, and continued studying after saying casually, "Probably Abhay didn't wake up today". When I asked why, he didn't reply.

Every hostel has at least one overly introvert guy. Abhay Gaur was the one in our hostel, a meticulous and neat fellow. Second year, Chemistry honours. He and his roommate, Aniket Mishra, lived in the neighbouring room number 3. Seeing him studying seriously, I did not insist on an answer and went to the bathroom for a bath. After all, it's not everyday that you get to use the bathroom immediately

after it has been cleaned afresh. My eyes for once just glanced at the clock on the wall – it was around exactly 9 AM.

Abhay's suicide note ran thus: "I just cannot take it anymore. My life is nothing but eternal suffering. I guess everyone's life is like that, but I don't chose to spend my precious life like this. My name, Abhay, means fearless. And fearless I shall be. There is no shame in the step I'm about to take. I feel proud that I have the power to do what I'm about to. Not everyone can do this. Especially alone, without any help. But it's a different matter that I don't need any help in doing what I must do. I know my parents will feel bad when the world gets to know. I am their only son after all. Even I feel bad. I was leading such a good life. I had so many dreams. If only things wouldn't have gone so wrong lately.... I have no other choice now. I'm ashamed of my past. But I won't let my past dominate my future. This is the only way that I can save my as well as my family's honour."

I will attempt to give a little description here. The dead body was found sitting on the chair, with a verical cut mark across his artery on the left arm. The blade with which it was done, was in his right arm, grasped rather lightly. His face resembled that of a man sleeping peacefully. His dark skin was unchanged, and his head leaned upon his chest. Both his arms were placed on the table, under which was the suicide note. The note was a page torn out of his diary, which was nearby on his bed. The handwriting was no doubt his.

Aniket had gone out of the hostel at 9:10 AM that day to attend classes in his college. We discovered the body at around 2 PM, when Subhash observed that Abhay, a man who so strictly followed his routine, did not show up even for lunch at the hostel mess. Subhash, I and a few others had then went to check on his

room. The door was closed, but not locked. Indrajit, Abhay's closest friend in the hostel, went in first. He could not believe what he was seeing. At first, he thought his friend was pranking him by sitting in such an eerie manner. I took Indrajit to my room, and tried to comfort him. He was crying – something hard to imagine on his tough face. After taking a good look (with a surpringly stern and emotionless

face), Subhash called in the police, then informed the hostel warden. The police came in about half an hour later. Abhay's body was sent for autopsy in the nearby Base hospital. Preliminary report would arrive in a day. The final report would take much longer. Aniket came back from college a little after 3 PM.

When he was informed about what had happened, he sadly, but calmly, admitted that Abhay was behaving a little depressed lately. He regretted that he could not make out that Abhay would have committed suicide. Indeed, Abhay was a kind of guy all of us knew to be someone who did not need anyone's help in anything. It was what he himself believed about himself. The officer-in-charge asked us a few very simple questions from us all who knew him. The police could not find any meaningful reason for the suicide. The best reason we could find is his consistent poor academic performance, and a breakup to a year-long relationship about a week ago. At last, the parents of the deceased were informed. I cannot imagine how they must have felt. All I know is that they rushed from Patna for Delhi at once, for I heard that by midnight they had seen the corpse, and began preparations for Abhay's last rites.

Life in a hostel is supposed to be the best part of one's life. At least that's what my father had told me. Ironically, someone I knew had ended his life in this supposed-to-be paradise. The entire hostel was sad.

Subhash had been acting very strange ever since the body was discovered. He was not talking to almost anyone in the hostel (I being the notable exception), and carried a constant grim expression on his face. It was hard to believe then that he might be traumatised too. Probably just out of the need for a little fresh air, he went out of the hostel for a stroll today morning for about an hour after breakfast, around 7:40 AM. But that was not the case – he was not traumatised at all. He was after something, as I got to know later.

At 10 AM, Subhash texted me: "Come quickly to the common room with as many people as possible". I was confused. And nervous too of what was going to happen, but I obeyed. The common room of our hostel was a quite small room, a cross breed of a library and an indoor games room. I could bring only about 10 people with me, including Aniket and Indrajit. Subhash was sitting alone in a corner when we entered,

thinking about something. As we entered, he stood up. "I have an announcement to make here right now," he said. "Make yourselves comfortable, and then we shall begin." When everyone was settled across the room, each one sitting in a chair turned towards the centre where he stood, Subhash began.

"Suicide," he said grimly, "is not just someone taking his own life. It is the culmination of a long process. This aspect of suicide is very less understood..." Two of the hostelites, who were going past the room at the moment, entered the room on seeing so many people assembled without the warden nearby.

"...It is true that Abhay was becoming increasingly irregular towards his end. But no one suspected that he would take his own life. The truth is, he did not. He was murdered." Absolute silence. No one could believe what they were hearing. And who they were hearing it from.

"We tend to think of suicide as an easy way out of the miseries of life. What we miss out is the fact that it takes courage. Slitting one's own wrist with a blade is not an easy thing to do. It involves the giving up of all attachments from life. Yet evidence points to Abhay's being able to do it in the first attempt, as well as

without any apparent reason for suicide. Interestingly, I observed that the entire suicide note did not contain even a single reference to words like suicide and death. It is a very poor suicide note, if it is one, which does not clearly state the reason, or who is to blame, or who is not to be. Thus Abhay's suicide note is a very bad one, or not a suicide note at all. Given the perfectionist that he was, the

former seems to be more improbable than the latter."

"So what was it then?", said Taranath, a senior of ours.

"A diary entry. The page was torn out of his diary, as we know. He had written it as a diary entry. It was his murderer who tore the page and placed it accordingly to create the illusion of a suicide note." Subhash's answer, however, still had a huge flaw.

"Abhay had clearly committed suicide. Are you saying that he wrote a diary entry, and then someone slit his wrist and fabricate a suicide?" I went on, "Even so, this method of suicide takes a certain amount of time to die, until he would have bled out to death. Are you suggesting that he just cooperated with his murderer?" "Not at all. And I am coming to that." Subhash said, "About an hour ago, I had a conversation with Mahesh. Ah yes, I'll take it that most of us here don't know his name – he is the sweeper guy. He had come to my room at his usual time for cleaning. You were in Indrajit's room then," he said, looking at me. " I asked him about what he had saw yesterday in Abhay's room while cleaning it. Apparently

many people have asked him the same, but no one figured out what was wrong. "What he said put in the last piece of the puzzle in place. He said that the room was very usual in appearance. Aniket was sitting on the side of his bed, tying up his shoes. Abhay was on that same place as we found him, although not as the

way we found him. He was sitting on his chair, his hands on the table lying over a piece of paper, with his right hand holding a ball pen in a precise grip. Additionally, he was breathing very heavily. Mahesh bhaiya understood that Abhay was sad, and that it would have been better not to have talked to him in

such a situation. The room cleaning record register was therefore signed, quite unusually, by Aniket. This last thing was noticed by me when I signed the register myself yesterday, as my room is just the next one.

"Another thing that is of quite interest is the fact that his hands were grasping a ball pen. The 'suicide note', with its thick letters, was clearly written by a gel pen. Hence I prove my point about murder. Now we can come to the point of how the murder was executed. "Aniket, can you answer a question of mine?", Subhash looked towards Aniket, "I wonder what you know about rocuronium?"

Aniket replied, puzzled, "What is that ?" Subhash shrugged his shoulders, then explained. "Rocuronium is a steroid-based neuromuscular-blocking drug, usually used in general anaesthesia. It paralyses all the muscles in the body. It is my firm belief that somehow Abhay was made to ingest this drug. The usual route of administering this drug is intravenous, or from he veins, and it's swallowing in any way can cause a bunch of hazardous side effects on a living person, like vomiting, slurred speech or even coma. But Abhay was already dead before such effects could have taken place. "I would make a confession here. Today morning, after breakfast, I had gone to the hospital to offer my condolences to Abhay's parents, as well as to get an idea of the direction in which the autopsy was heading. It was by sheer luck, I must say, that I found out that a component of general anaesthesia was missing from a surgeon's stores there on the day before yesterday, when I overheard a conversation between two medical students. So the anaesthetic was stolen, directly or indirectly, by our murderer." Everyone's eyes were fixed on him. All but two minds in the entire room were confused.

"But let's get back to the topic. Once the drug would have got to work, Abhay would have become paralysed. Although he would have felt light headed, he could have roughly realised what was happening, but could do nothing. "The drug couldn't have been in his food, for all our meals are made in the hostel

mess. Therefore, it was in his water. Since just 0.6 mg of this drug is enough to induce a paralysis of at least 45 minutes, it would have left absolutely no trace on the now-empty water bottle. The murderer added the drug in the water bottle before Abhay would have got up in the morning. The drug would start working

within two minutes of Abhay's drinking water. Presumably Abhay was in the habit of drinking water after getting up or before having breakfast." Now Aniket asked the question which was in all our minds for the past few moments – "how are you jumping to this rocuronium bromide thing?" "I'm surprised how well you could pronounce the name of the drug in the first go, and also know it's full name," Subhash said. "As far as I know, none of the subjects you study in college has anything to do with general anaesthesia." Aniket looked angrily at Subhash. "Abhay committed suicide. You are overthinking too much now." His face had turned red.

"Rocuronium Bromide," replied Subhash, completely ignoring Aniket's last remark, "is known for increasing pulmonary vascular resistance. In simple words, it decreases the flow of blood from the heart to other parts of the body. When Abhay was under the effect of the anaesthetic, any cut on his body would have led to lower than usual loss of blood. "A little less important is the fact that while it is active, the drug has a particular side-effect on people who have asthma, like Abhay. Difficulty in breathing. This side-effect and Mahesh's account of Abhay's heavy breathing match perfectly. That is the importance of rocuronium in all this. I'll assume that the murderer had no idea about this side effect. "However, the ingenuity of this murderer lies in the fact of his play with timing. The post-mortem report would clearly put the time of death at around 9:35 AM. Which would put the time of Abhay's cutting his wrist in case of suicide between 9:20 AM and 9:25 AM, owing to the fact that death in this kind of suicide occurs within 10-15 minutes. The time of suicide thus indicated was when Abhay was alone in the room, since Aniket goes out of the hostel at 9:10 AM. For this, Aniket has two perfect alibis – the Security Guard who was on duty at the time at the main gate as well as the hostel check-out register. But owing to the thing about

pulmonary vascular resistance caused out of the anaesthetic, the actual cut could be inflicted just a little before 9:10 AM which would cause death around 9:35 -" Suddenly, Aniket got up from his chair and charged with all his might at Subhash. Subhash was prepared, but his physique was nothing compared to Aniket, who landed a punch on his face. Subhash fell. Aniket would have continued, but I andthe others quickly went and tightly grasped him. Knowing that it was over, Aniket didn't resist frantically for too long. "I'm calling the police," said Indrajit. He had finally regained his composure now. Subhash got up. "No," he said, "wait". He went up to where the boys were holding Aniket tightly. Aniket was giving him a very vicious stare. Subhash gave a nice blow of his fist on Aniket's head. Aniket grunted in pain, and then lost consciousness. "Now you may call the police," Subhash said. "And yes, someone inform the

warden too. This, my friends, is the murderer of Abhay Gaur." A long silence followed. I broke it after what seemed like an eternity, by asking Subhash, "how could this anaesthetic go undetectable in a post-mortem?"

Subhash looked at me with a smile. His nose was bleeding from the punch he had received from Aniket. His spectacles were miraculously intact. "Good observation", he said. Then he explained, "once rocuronium bromide's effect ends, the only minute traces of it left is found in the liver, which is in no way related to the slitting of one's artery in the wrist. These minute traces get even more insignificant by time, owing to its half-life of about one-and-a-half hours." "A question still remains," commented Subhash after some time, "that of the motive. It is not very clear, but I know what it is. Probably. Let the police interrogate him and find out for a certainty. They can do this job better than me." The police interrogation of Aniket Mishra led to us knowing of why he killed Abhay.

Both these men, Abhay and Aniket, were very talented students. But eventually they were misguided by some of their peers and got involved into petty politics of hooliganism. They were among a vast group of young people who were the pawns of morally corrupt politicians. They were assigned all kinds of jobs – arson, extortion, smuggling, beating people. However, Abhay was not made for such a life at all. The more he immersed in it, the more he felt the heavy weight of guilt on his shoulders. Over time, this started

taking a toll on him – his behaviour, his relationships, his academic potential – every aspect of his life. So, when his girlfriend dumped him, he realised that he was on a wrong path, and could not continue down it anymore. This thought of his became a conviction when he discovered just two days before his death that

they were being used as an instrument for instigating a major communal riot right here in Delhi. He just could not do it anymore. He told his roommate – who was one of the few friends he had – about his

decision to surrender to the police and tell them everything that he knows about the riots that would have taken place. Aniket found this change in Abhay's mind very surprising, and tried to talk him out of it. But Abhay was determined of his choice.

That night, Aniket went out in the evening for a jogging. He smuggled rocuronium bromide into the hostel in his own empty water bottle on his way back to hostel through the hospital complex. In this, he was helped by one of the janitors of the hospital.

The problem that day was created mainly because Abhay had woken up later than usual, as he was to go to the police station and not college. He woke up at 8:40 AM, and brushed his teeth, after which he drank a little water and then sat on his chair to see for once his yesterday's diary entry. It was then that the anaesthetic started its effect. So far, Aniket had just thought about perfectly fabricating a

suicide, but on seeing the open page of the diary before him, he had the idea of creating the illusion of a suicide note as well....

The police have taken due action. All the potential rioters have been arrested. Many rackets have been busted. As for Aniket, the District Court is to give its verdict on his fate tomorrow.

In a way, Subhash's intervention avoided a major communal riot. A nice way to begin our adventures together, I think.

CHAPTER SEVEN

Author's Interview – Beth Gardner

Author Beth Gardner

Q1. Tell us a bit about yourself.

I did self-fund my education at Drexel University graduating in 3-years. I self-funded my career in Rowing. Growing up with a special needs older sibling who had cerebral palsy and one lung helped to motivate me to be self reliant and a go getter in life.

Q2. How did publishing your first book change your process of writing?

I was put into school starting at age 4 turning 5. In the USA you don't put children into the 1st grade until age 6 turning 7 because at that age children's brains are developed enough to handle the academics. I was too you being out into the 1st grade and I struggled emotionally for it. These two teachers in this post helped me significantly. I love teachers.

Q3. If you could tell your younger writing self, anything, and what would it be?

I would tell my younger self to continue going to the library to read books. It is what Ron Beebe and Mrs. Wolfe mentioned in the above post recommended to my parents. And it helped tremendously! It changed the trajectory of my university and career paths. I did not study journalism in University. I never set out to write a book in life. As I mentioned in that video, because I was journaling when I was receiving my cancer treatment, I realized that I had content for a book. Journaling was recommended to me by the oncology nurses. Very wise of them to recommend that. I finished the book in 2004. I explained in the video why it took sooooo long for me to publish it.

Q4. What does literary success look like to you?

It means motivating, influencing human beings globally to strive for their passions in life. It shows readers, the actual miracles God can create in your life. Bottom line: follow your God given gifts and passions in life.

Q5. Does your family support your career as a writer?

I come from a family that does not talk much about their accomplishments. My mother is from Swedish heritage. Her family from Sweden, Lutheran Religion of Christianity, came to the USA in 1900. In the Swedish culture, you don't boast, talk about your accomplishments. It's looked down upon.

Q6. What one thing would you give up to become a better writer?

I live a very non-materialistic, modest life. I eat a limited diet. So, I don't have much to "give up." For me to become a better writer, I would take writing courses specific to where I need improvement.

Q7. Who's your Inspiration in the literary field?

I grew up in a home where reading the newspaper was required. We also had subscriptions to Time Magazine. Newspaper journalists inspire me because they are required to write in a highly pressured industry. Their articles need to be spot on without any grammatical errors. To me, that's a VERY impressive gift from good to be able to do that. I worked at Www.Philly.com during the last year of my Rowing career. I was in charge of helping to build the website restaurant database in Philadelphia and posting articles from the Entertainment page of the Philadelphia Inquirer onto Philly.com's pages. I was so impressed with the caliber of writing the journalists had. I am impressed with the Wall Street Journal and New York

Times journalists also. It's an incredible skill to be able to write true live stories under a pressure cooker type of environment.

Q8. What kind of research do you do, and how long do you spend researching before beginning a book?

I am by nature VERY resourceful because of having to grow up quickly in life due to having a role model like my late special needs brother Todd. My parents trained me to be a "do-it-yourselfer" kid. At the age of 16, I was in charge of buying my own clothing including athletic apparel and running shoes. I earned money from babysitting after school and on weekends. I have an entrepreneurial spirit. I paid for my Drexel University education in Philadelphia, PA. It cost me $14,000 a year. I graduated in 3-years to avoid paying another $14,000.

Q9. What's the turning point of your life when you realize you want to be an author?

I don't come from a family dynamic whereby the MALE is believed to be the breadwinner. BOTH the husband and wife share financial responsibilities. I was inspired to be an independent female by my beloved paternal grandmother, Martha Clark Gardner. See Instagram posts. Her father was a successful attorney in Pittsburgh. She grew up with 3-sisters who all went to Carnegie Mellon University. Her parents could afford it and believed in the early 1900's that women she educated. My parents did not earn much money. We lived a very modest lifestyle. Education and being involved in extracurricular activities (sports) was paramount in my family, so that was what we focused on. In addition, being spiritually fed was important. We attended Christian church every Sunday and lived in a predominantly Jewish community. I learned about both religions growing up. I was fortunate to have that exposure and to NOT be discriminatory to other religions.

Q10. How long on average does it take you to write a book?

wrote the book between 2001 to 2004 when working full-time in the investment industry and as Co-founder of Row for the Cure Philadelphia. See attached resume for ALL Cancer Non-profit past work.